PAUL GAUGUIN

'Barbarism is for me a rejuvenation.'

PAUL GAUGUIN

PAUL GAUGUIN

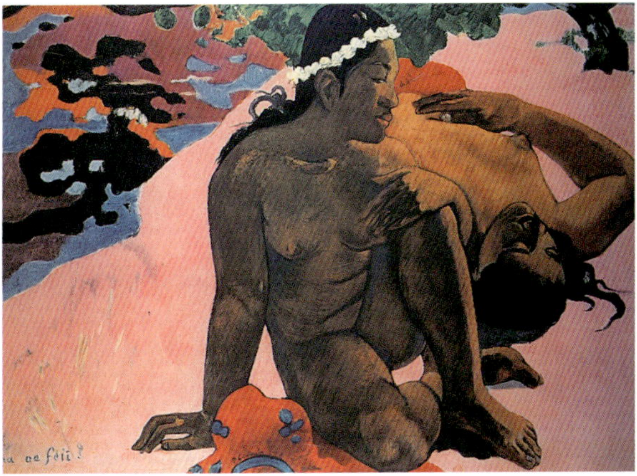

BROCKHAMPTON PRESS
LONDON

TITLE PAGE

AHA OE FEII? (WHAT, ARE YOU JEALOUS?), 1892.

Gauguin was inspired by the beauty of the women of Tahiti, thinking they possessed 'a certain something, penetrating and infinitely mysterious.' Gauguin presents them as natural and unselfconscious - a primitive Eve.

PAUL GAUGUIN (1848-1903), painter, sculptor and printmaker, has with Cezanne and Van Gogh, been seen to be one of the founders of modern art.

Gauguin was born in Paris, the son of a journalist and mother of Spanish-Peruvian descent. Spending his early childhood in Peru, he returned to France and, aged 17, seeking adventure, joined the French Merchant Navy. After six years of seafaring, he worked for a Paris stockbroking company, where he was very successful. In 1873 he met and married a young Danish girl, Mette Gad, and settled down to a conventional middle class family life. He began to paint in his spare time, encouraged by Pissarro and influenced by the Impressionists in general. In 1883, aged 35, whether by resignation or dismissal, he left his job, financial security and then his family to entirely devote himself to art.

Spending periods at Pont-Aven and Le Pouldu in Brittany, he became fascinated by the daily life and religion of the Breton peasants, 'Natural Man' as he called them. The primitive feel to his surroundings corresponded with his artistic aspirations. He became dissatisfied with the restraints of Impressionism and so freed himself from its naturalism, evolving a new style. He painted from life but also from his imagination or memory, using colour and design both expressively and symbolically. Visually utilising folk art, medieval art and stained glass, he stylistically developed the use of flat planes of pure colour and strongly outlined forms. The influence of the Japanese print can be seen in his rejection of aerial and linear perspective and use of arabesques, contributing to the decorative appeal of his work.

He was not alone in his move against purely representational art. His allies were the 'Symbolists' and another group of artists, the 'Nabis', who worked with him in Brittany. He also shared ideas with his friend Vincent van Gogh until this friendship ended dramatically after a three month visit in Arles in 1888.

Disenchanted with the 'civilised life' that gave him neither money nor recognition, Gauguin left for Tahiti in the South Seas in 1891, in his search of the primitive life and a return to innocence. Some of his best work was produced here. He painted idealised, poetic scenes of native life, set against the tropical landscape. His canvases were powerful with particularly rich and exotic colours, incorporating symbols, Christian themes and dark and disturbing images to represent the folklore, religion and superstitions of the people.

After briefly returning to France, he settled permanently in Polynesia from 1895 until his death in Atuana, in the Marquesas Islands in 1903. Although he had suffered increasingly from poverty, ill-health and isolation, this was not reflected in his work. His paintings are still seen by many to be as fresh and beautiful as when they were first painted.

Madeleine Bernard, 1888. *right*

This pensive portrait was painted when Madeleine, aged 17, visited Pont-Aven with her mother. He was introduced to her by her brother, Emile Bernard, the theorist and painter, whose enthusiasm and ideas acted as a catalyst for Gauguin's new artistic direction.

Landscape in Brittany, 1888. *overleaf*

In painting this rural village scene, Gauguin shows early signs of a style 'synthetism', whereby he simplifies the line and colour to create greater impact.

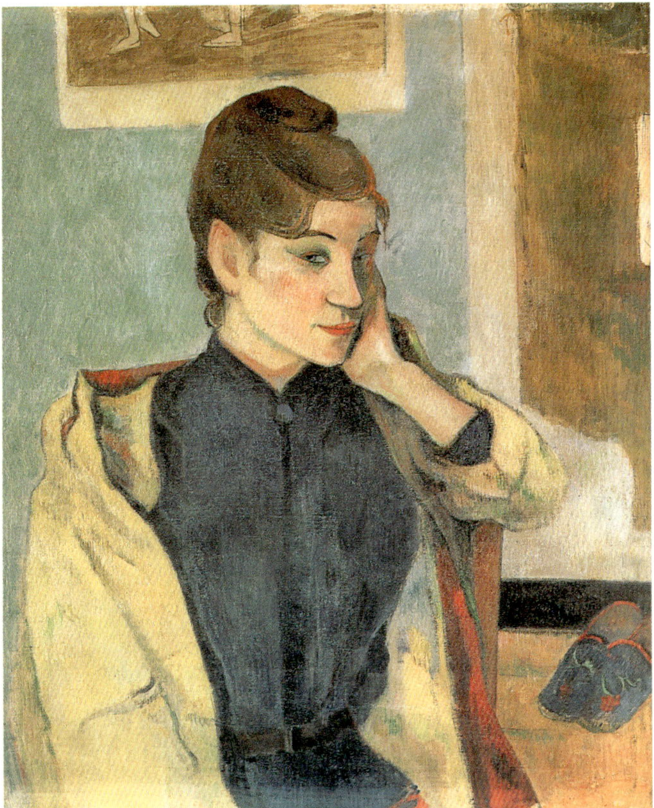

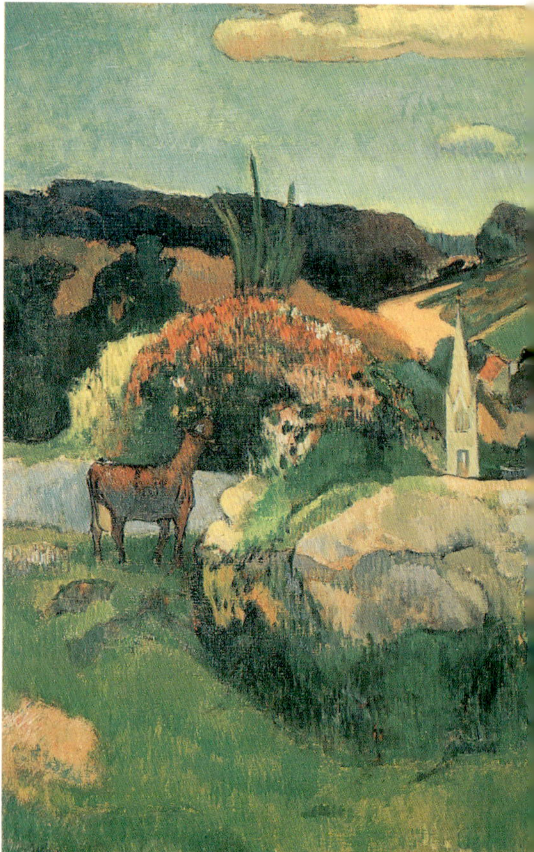

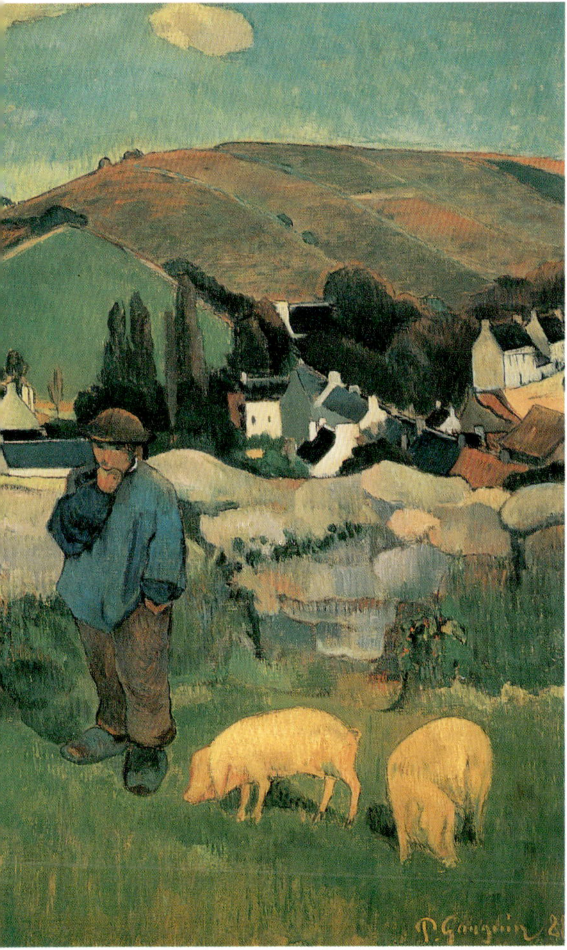
P. Gauguin 88

Gauguin 88

Les Alyscamps, 1888. *left*

Painted during his short stay with Van Gogh, both artists were to depict this autumnal scene at the necropolis in Arles. In Gauguin's version there is a free use of red, yellow and blue and the paints are thinly applied. He also includes the ghost like figures of three women.

In the Cafe de la Gare, 1888. *overleaf*

This painting was seen as a, conscious or otherwise, homage to his friend, Van Gogh. Gauguin paints the same cafe and uses the same models (Madam Ginoux, the proprietor in the foreground and Roulin the postman and the Zouave in the background). He also uses the same aggressive palette of red, green and ochre as his companion. However, his more controlled painting has a sense of detachment.

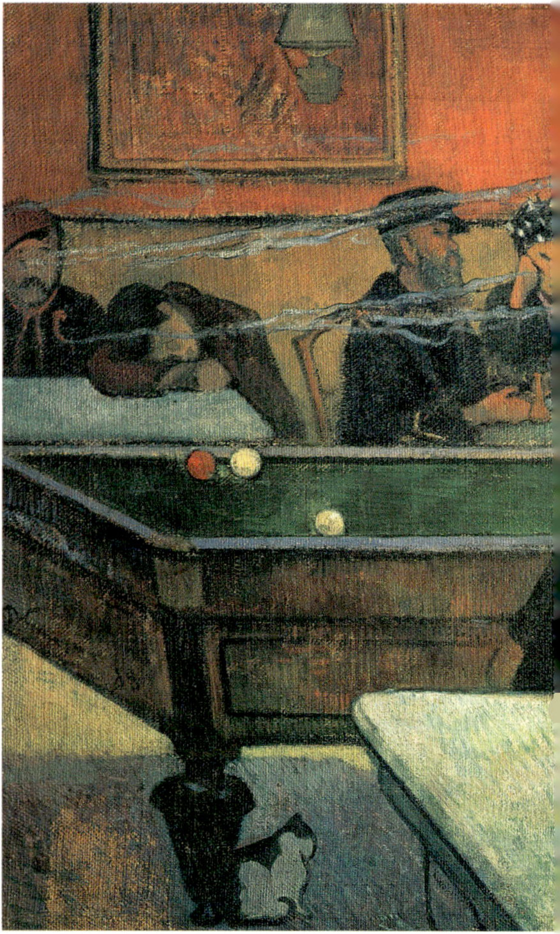

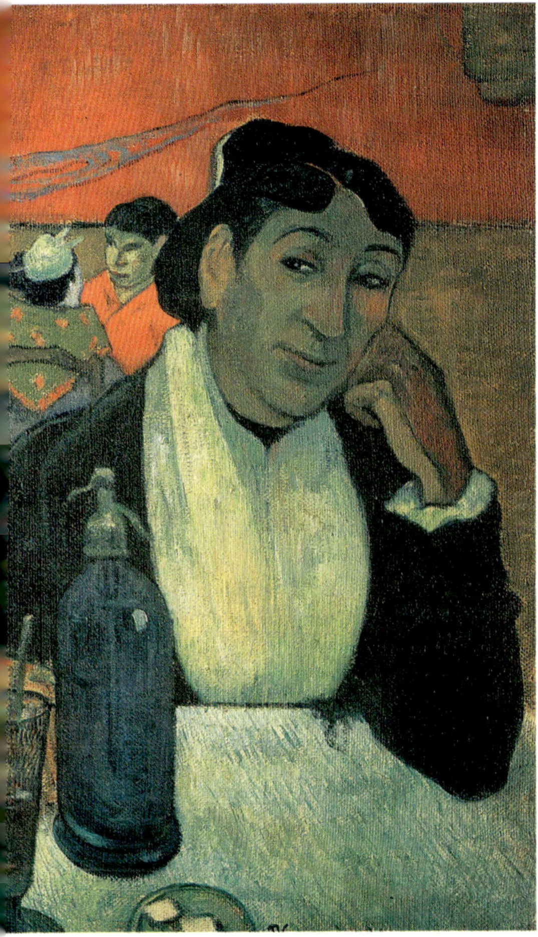

FEMALE NUDE IN WAVES, 1889 *right*

This torturous image with symbolic and sexual overtones, whilst having affinity with Impressionism, through its emotive power clearly shows Gauguin as a forerunner of Expressionism.

GRAPE HARVEST IN ARLES - HUMAN MISERY, 1888. *overleaf* Working partly from memory, Gauguin painted onto sackcloth instead of canvas. The seated, hunched, brooding figure, was used again in later paintings, as a pose representing suffering and despair. It was based on sketches he made of a Peruvian mummy seen in a Paris museum.

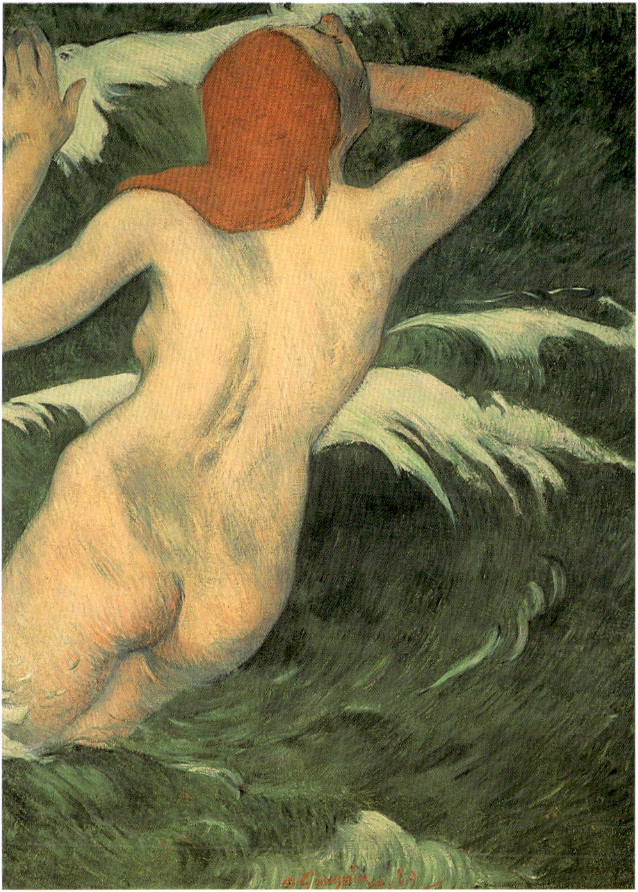

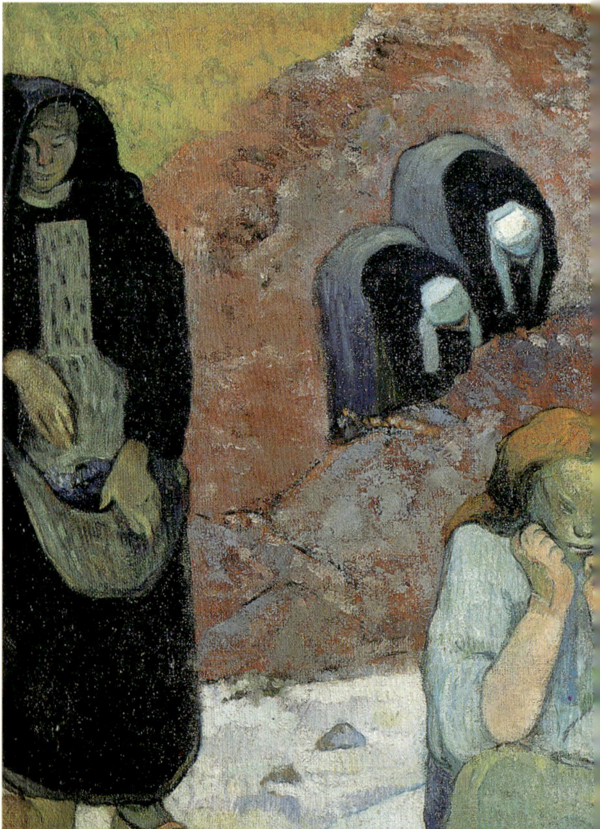

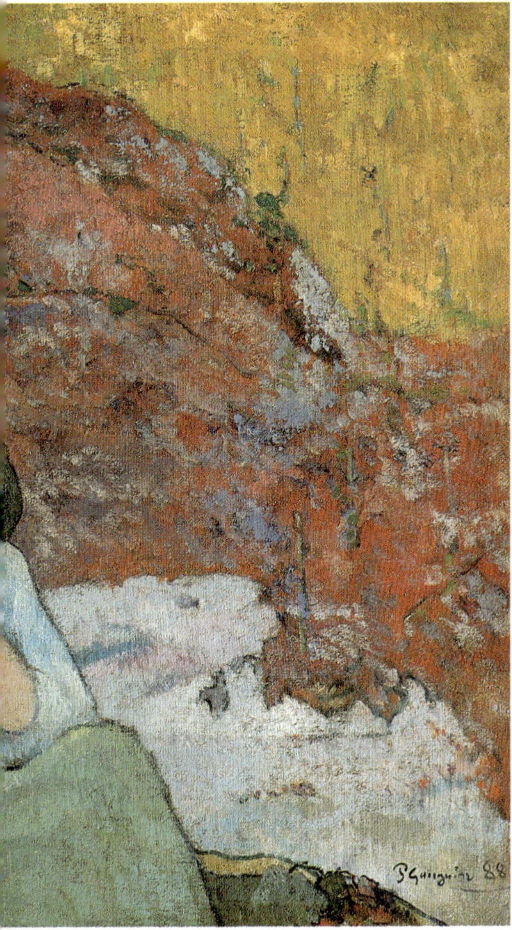
P Gauguin 88

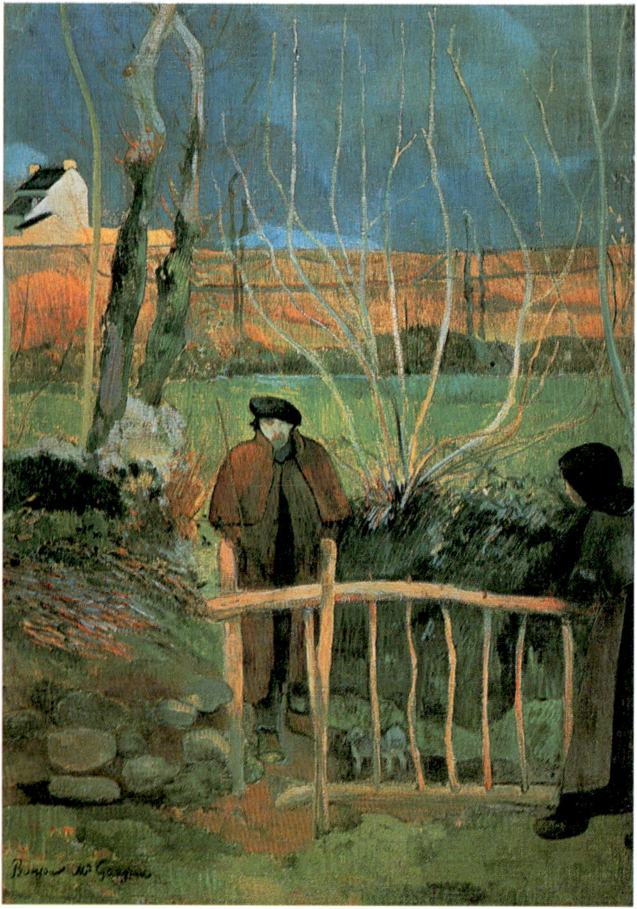

Bonjour Monsieur Gauguin, 1889. *left*

This self-portrait inspired by Courbet's famous *Bonjour Monsieur Courbet*, is based on the theme of the artist as a lonely wanderer. It conveys a mood of depression and isolation.

Breton Seaweed Collectors, 1889. *overleaf*

Painted at Le Pouldu in the biting cold of December, Gauguin uses darker colours and exaggerates the women's poses and hands to suggest the tedium of physical labour against the harsh elements.

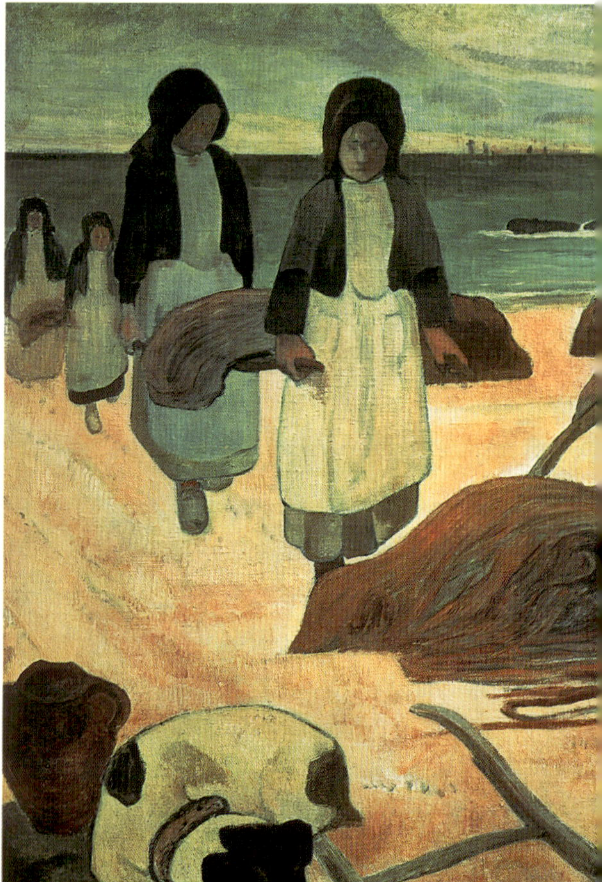

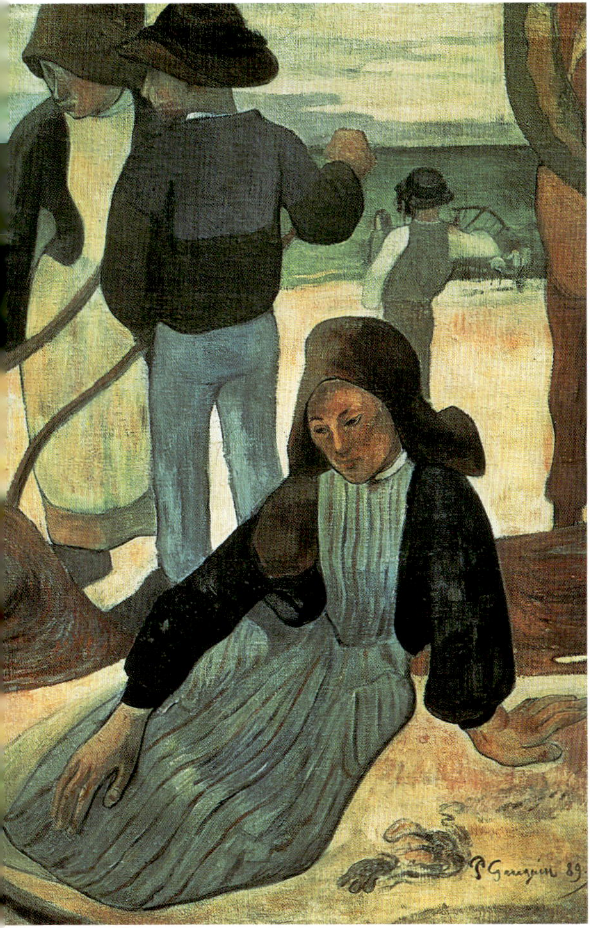
P Gauguin 89

Breton Landscape with Haystack, 1890. *right*
The transformation of a simple rustic scene into a field of brilliantly non-representational colours anticipates later developments in his Tahitian pictures.

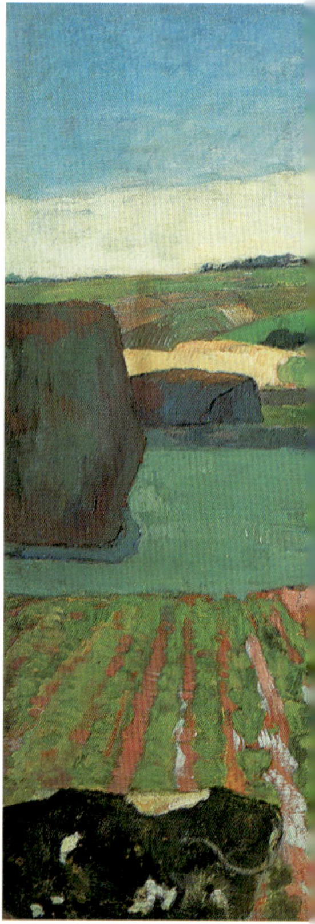

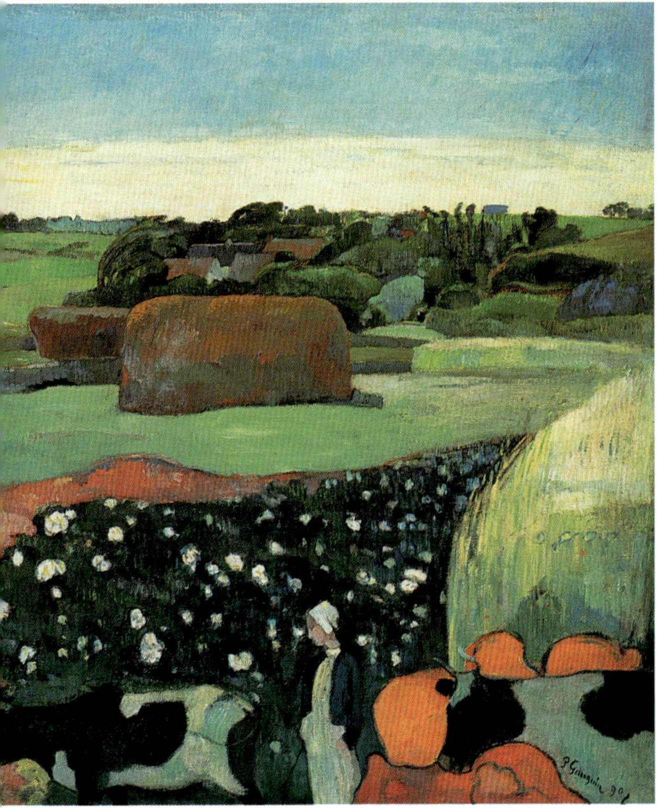
P Gauguin 90

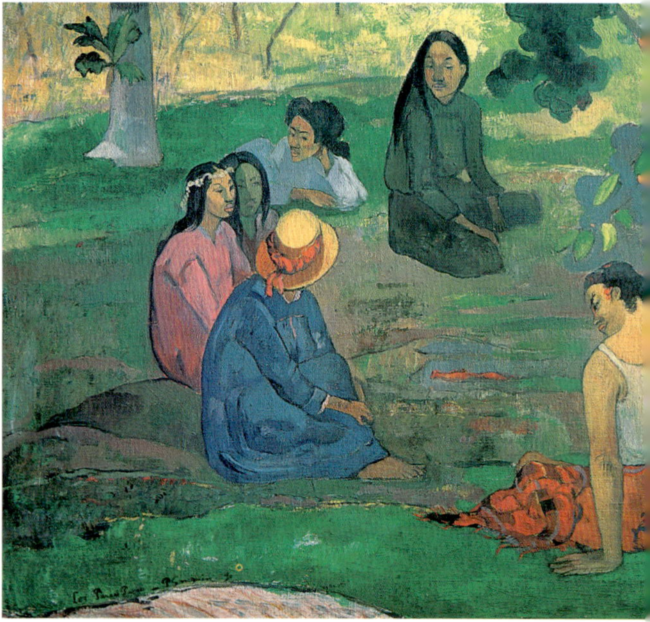

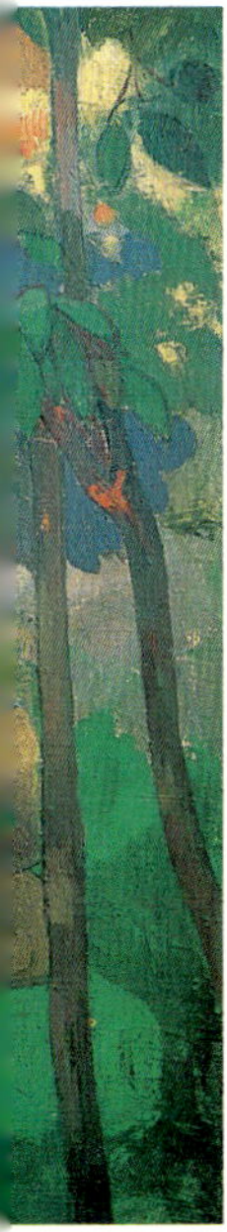

THE CONVERSATION, 1891. *left*

Despite its tropical background, this early Tahitian painting reflects the Europeanization of the island, shown in the natives' style of modest dress. He later moved to a remoter part of the island.

THE MEAL OR THE BANANAS, 1891.

overleaf This is an example of his interest in combining figure and still life subjects into one composition. The arrangement of the tablecloth, knife and fruit echoes those in a still life by Cezanne that Gauguin owned and admired.

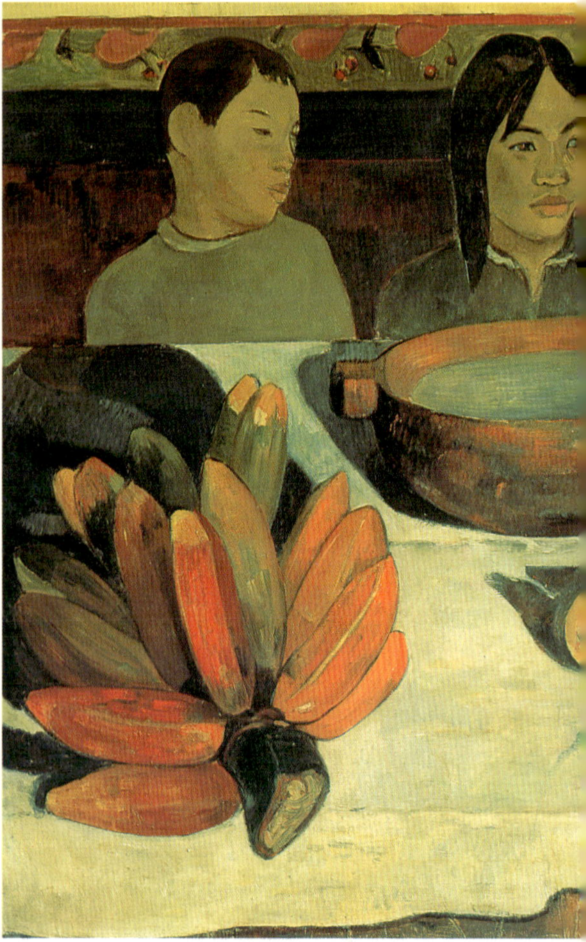

P. Gauguin 91

THE WOODCUTTER OR MAN WITH AN AXE, 1891. *right*

He simplifies colour into broad areas, broken up by arbitrary arabesques, which Gauguin likened to the characters of an 'unknown, mysterious language'. His woodcutter seems to epitomize the image of the 'noble savage'.

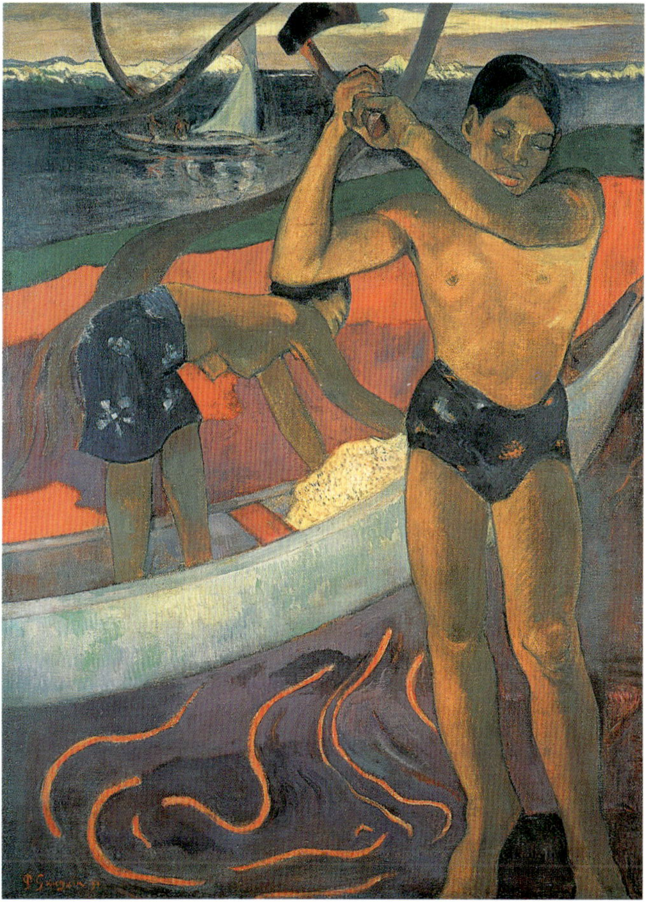

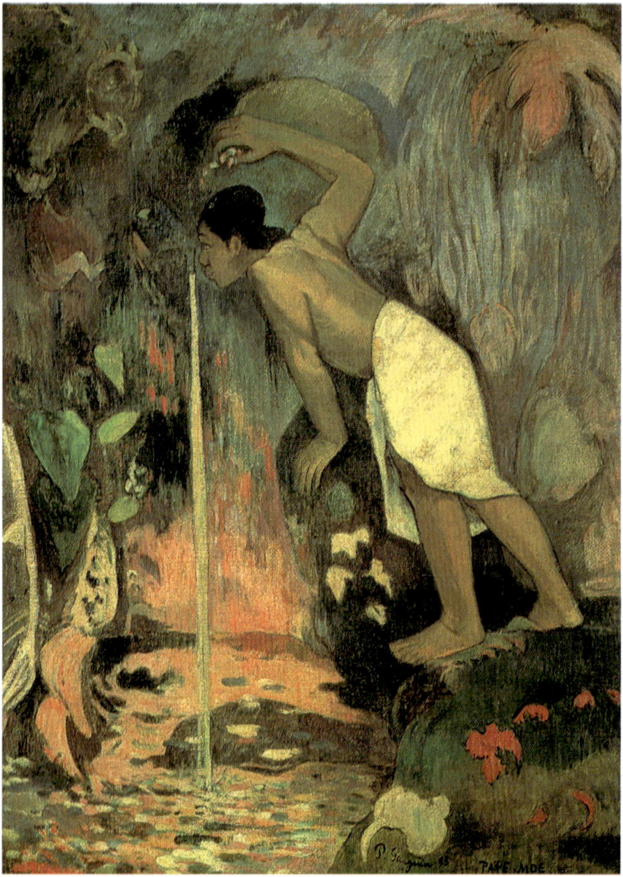
PAPE MOE

Pape Moe (Mysterious Waters), 1893. *left*

By travelling into wilder area of Tahiti less touched by the French influence, Gauguin felt he had found the 'real Tahiti'. His compositions were to revive this 'Paradise lost'. In this picture, evocative colours add mystery to this scene.

Breton Women, 1894. *overleaf*

Painted during his last nostalgic return to Brittany, he again depicts a familiar theme of Breton women in traditional dress. A tension is created in the painting by the feeling of a conspiracy between the figures in the foreground.

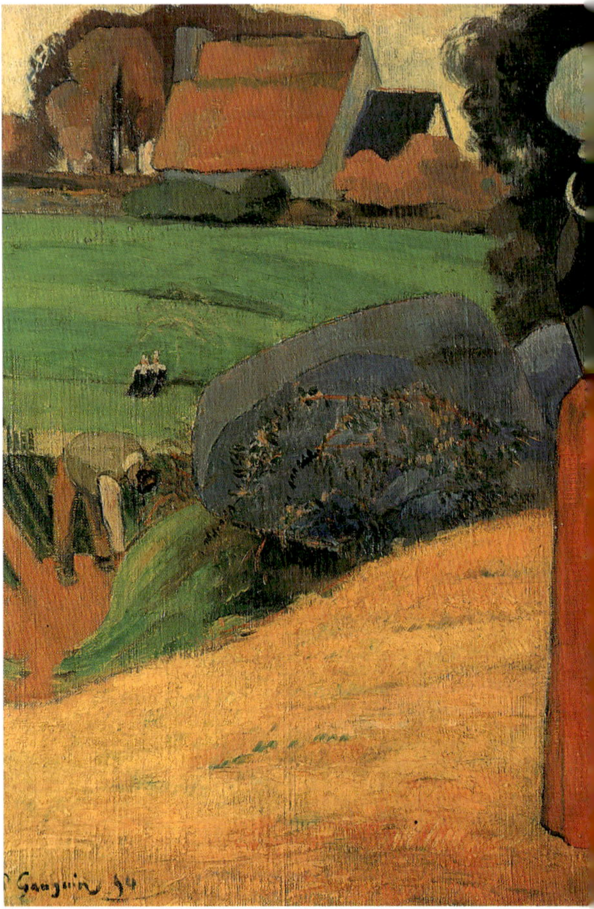
P Gauguin 94

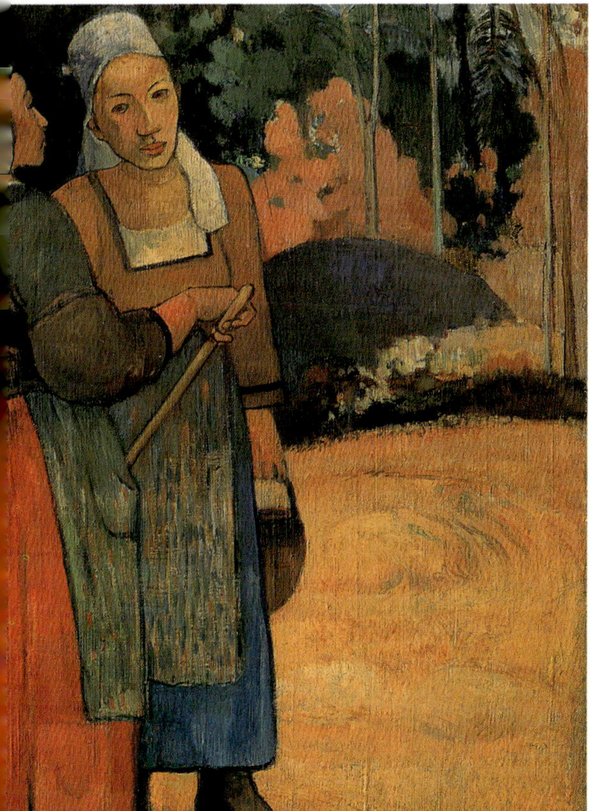

MAHANA NO ATAU

(DAY OF THE GOD), 1894.

Painted on his return to France, this painting unites many elements from earlier Tahitian work, and shows an imagined ancient Tahitian religious ritual. The brightly coloured organic shapes contrast with the formality of the composition. Worshippers are arranged symmetrically around the central idol, probably representing the god Hina.

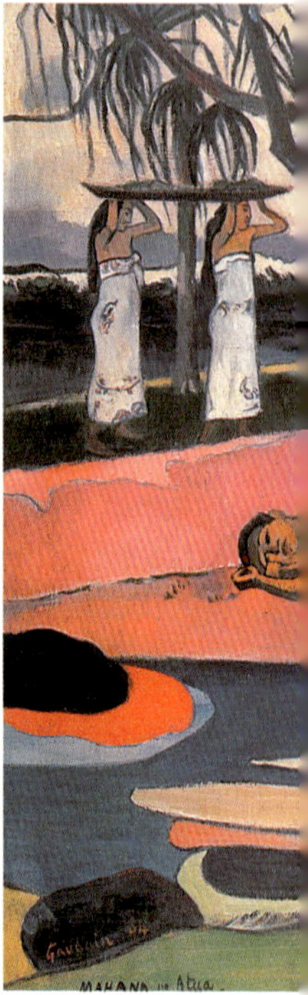

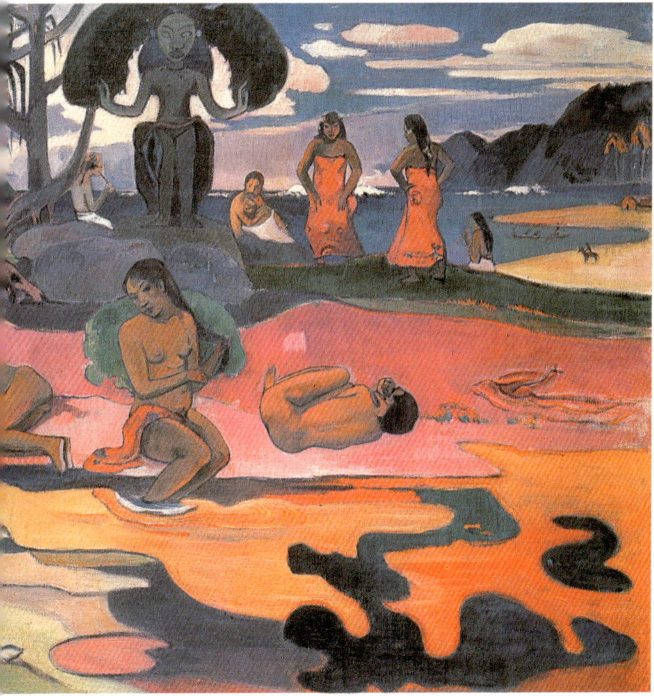

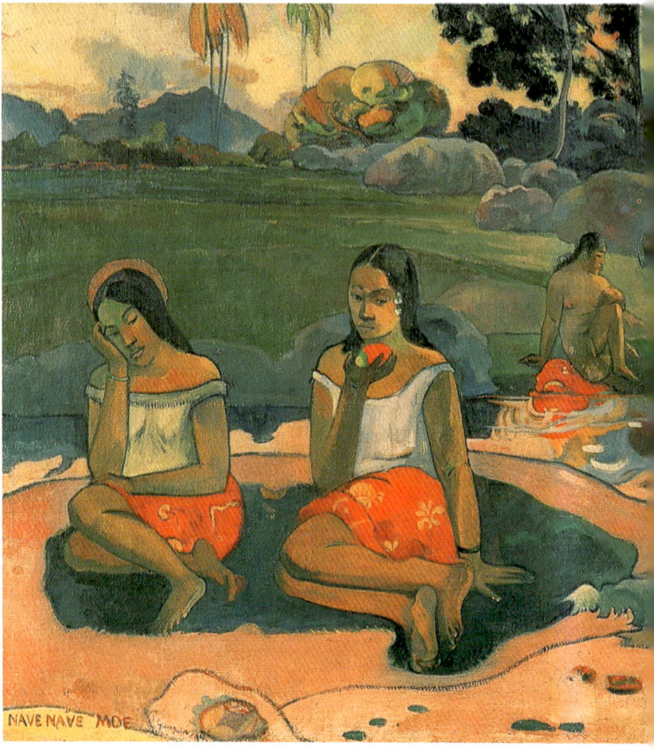
NAVE NAVE MOE

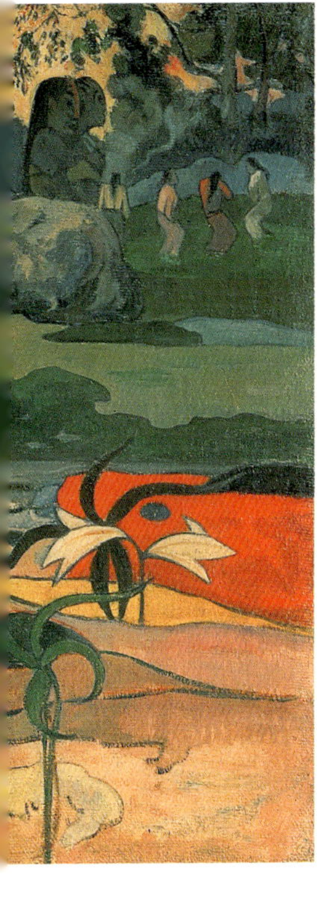

NAVE NAVE MOE

(DELICIOUS WATER), 1894.

A similar religious ritual in enacted in the background of this painting. As years of colonial rule had destroyed the indigenous religious practises and eroded Tahitian customs, Gauguin sought to resurrect them through his paintings. He emphasised the primitive and exotic nature of his work by giving them allusive Maori titles.

Portrait of young girl, Jeanne Goupil, 1896.

right Commissioned as a result of a temporary friendship with the island's lawyer Goupil, Gauguin produced a charming and delicately painted portrait capturing the sitter's youthful innocence.

Te Vaa (The Canoe), 1896. *overleaf*

A Tahitian version of picture inspired by *The Poor Fisherman* by Pierre Puvis de Chavannes, which Gauguin greatly admired.

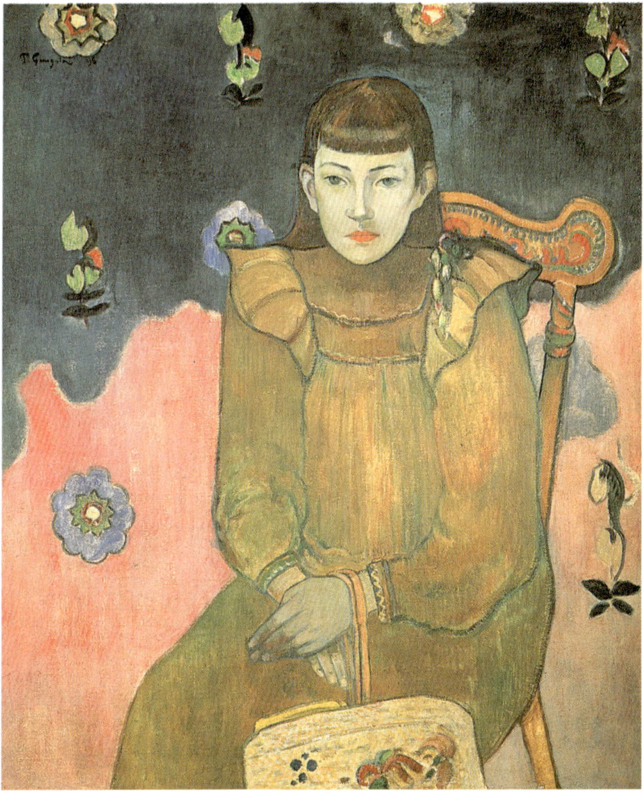

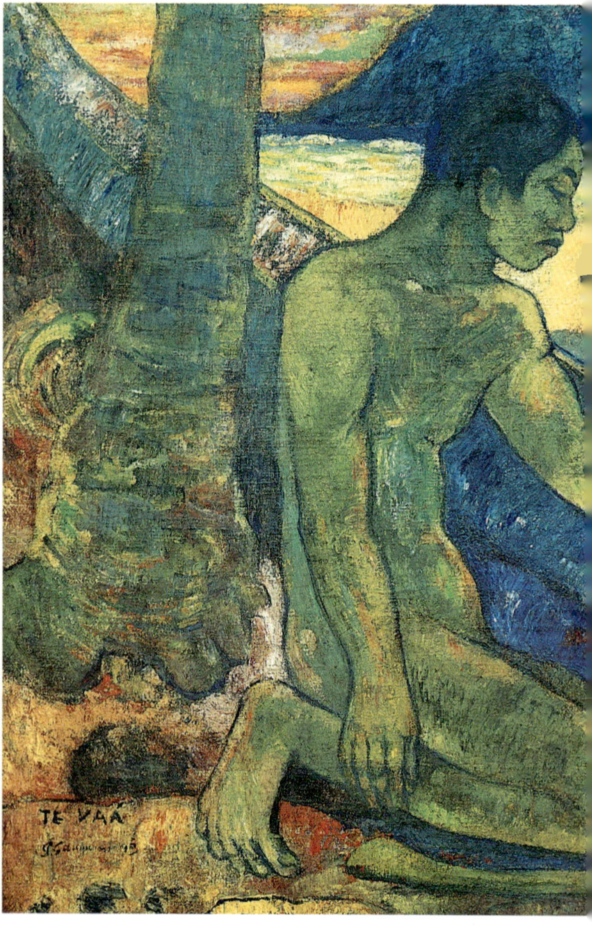
TE VAA

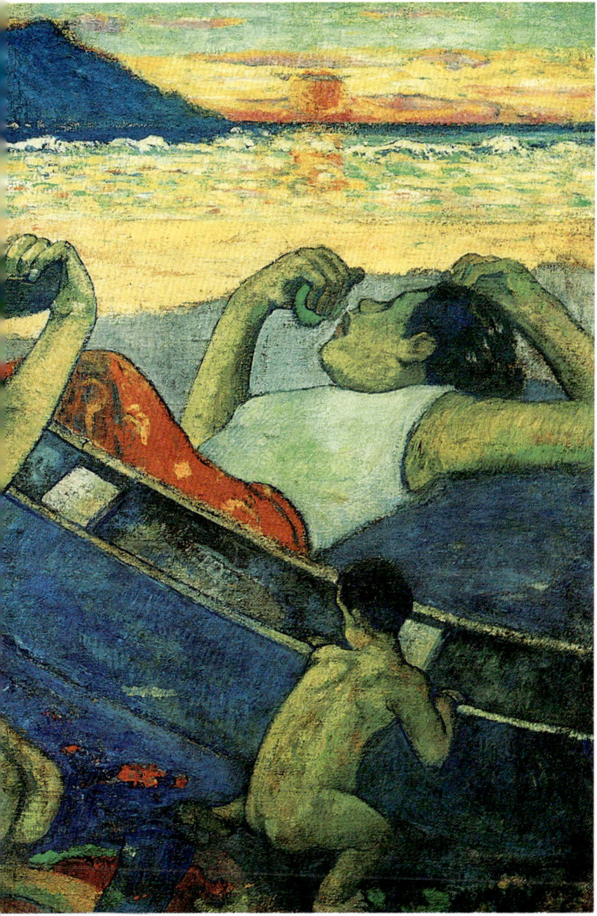

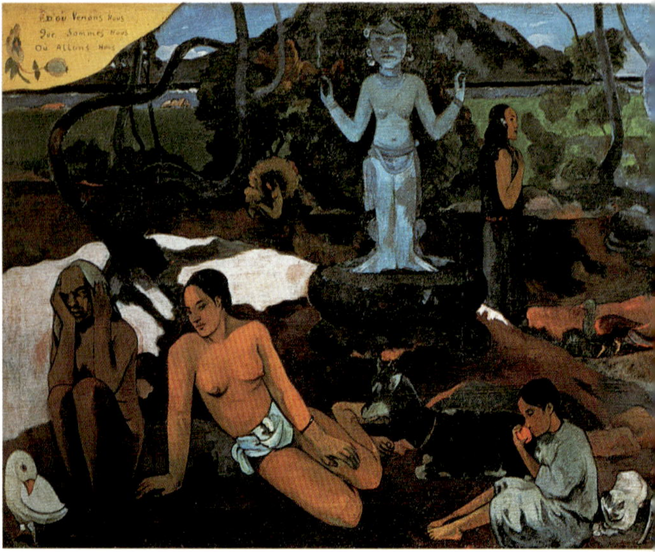

WHERE ARE WE FROM? WHAT ARE WE? WHERE ARE WE GOING?, 1897. *above*

Gauguin produced this monumental painting as a spiritual testament, shortly before attempting suicide. The picture reads from right to left and its theme is that of birth, life and death. Many figures had featured in previous paintings.

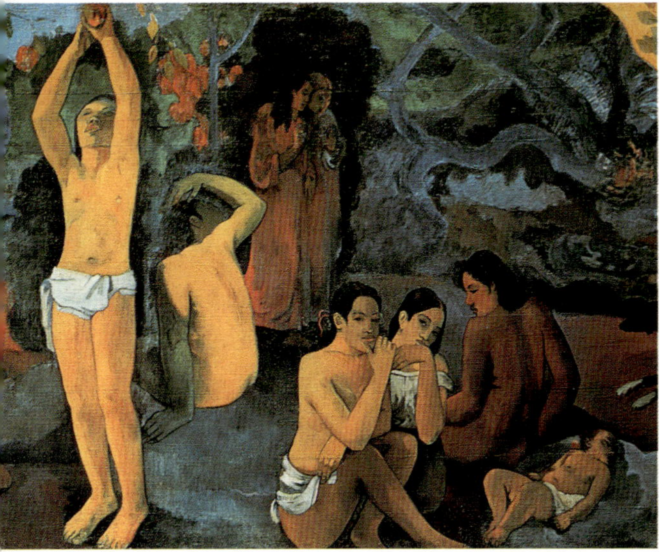

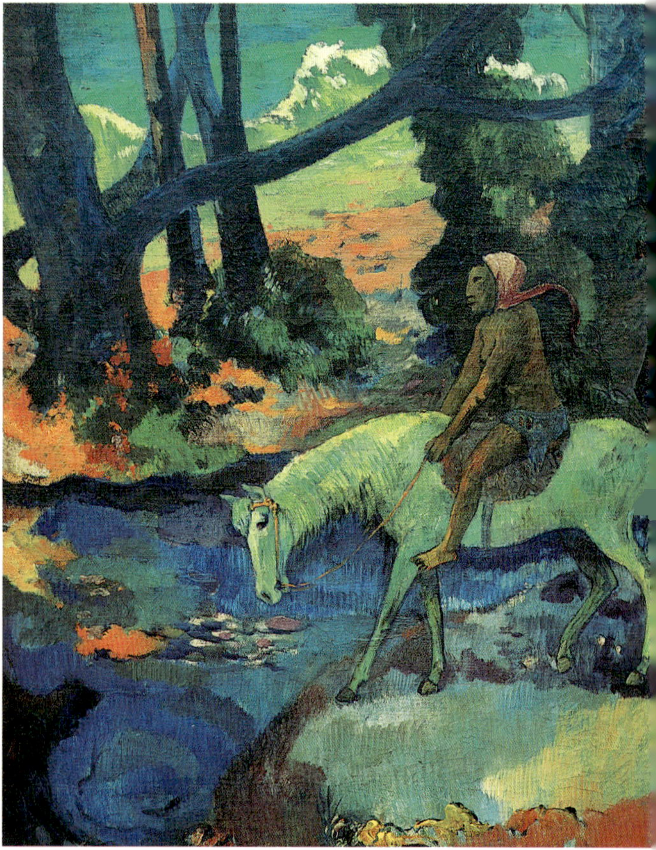

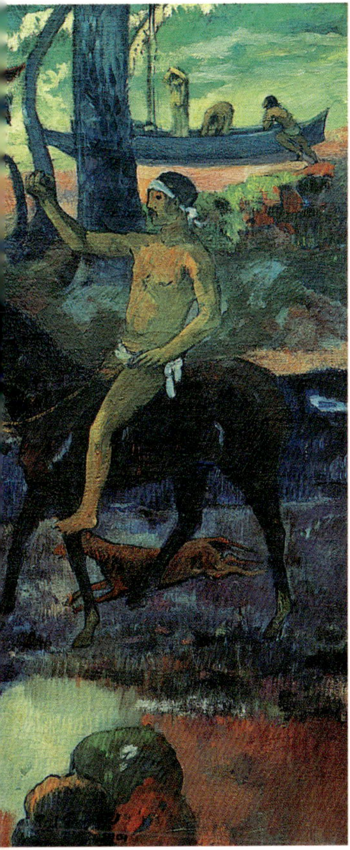

THE FORD OR THE FLIGHT

left In this painting he appears to have drawn his inspiration from Durer's engraving Knight, Death and the Devil, a copy of which he owned. The hooded figure symbolises death in an otherwise barbaric view of Arcadia.

Primitive Tales, 1902. *right*

The demonic figure to the left, perhaps representing a European intruder, is friend Meyer de Hann from Brittany. The painting evokes a mood that is exotic and mysterious. The red haired model is Tohotua (as seen again in *Lady with Fan*).

Still Life with Parrots, 1902. *overleaf*

The figure of Buddha, which presumably symbolizes Gauguin's own Buddist beliefs, gives an oriental flavour to this still life influenced again by Cezanne.

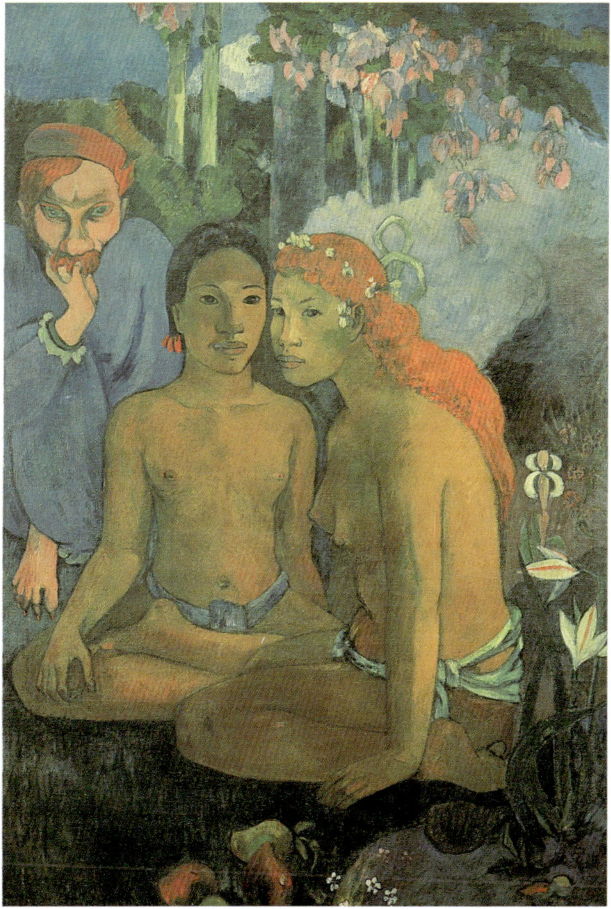

Paul
Gauguin
1902

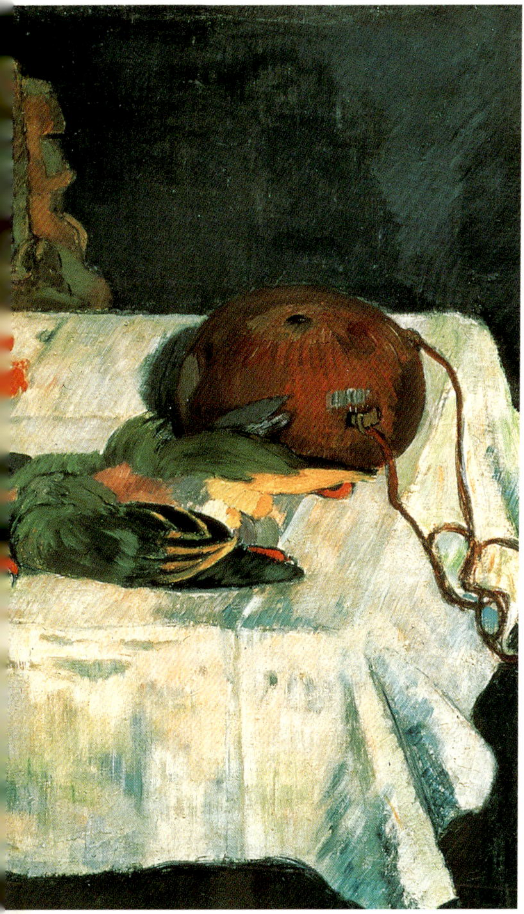

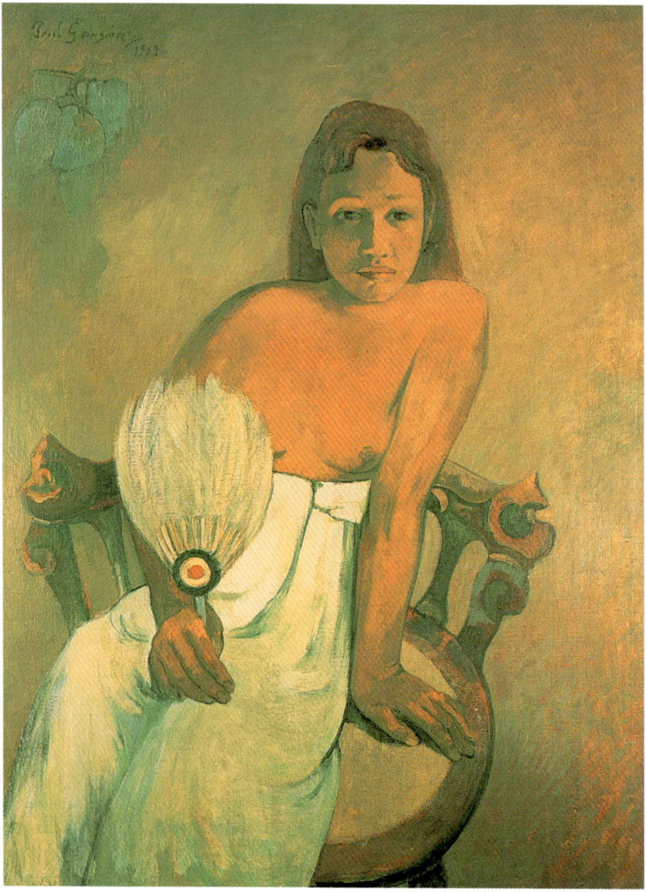

Young Woman with Fan, 1902. *left*

Using the same model, Tohotua, *(Primitive Tales)* the painting is based on a photograph of a woman taken in 1901 and found in Gauguin's hut after his death. The painting differs from the photograph in that it is more erotic and provocative. He represents an image of an archetypal Tahitian woman as being passive and sexually available.

FURTHER READING

Gauguin in the South Seas, Bengt Danielsson, London, 1965.

Studies in Post-Impressionism, John Rewald, London, 1986.

Gauguin, Belinda Thomson, Thames and Hudson, 1987.

PICTURE COLLECTIONS

Aha oe Feii? (What, are you jealous?) Pushkin Museum, Moscow. **Madeleine Bernard,** Musee de Pienture et de Sculpture, Grenoble. **Landscape in Brittany,** Collection of Lucille Ellis Simon, Los Angeles. **Les Alyscamps,** Galerie du Jeu de Paume, Paris. **In the Cafe de la Gare,** Pushkin Museum, Moscow. **Female Nude in Waves,** Cleveland Museum of Art, Cleveland, Ohio. **Bonjour Monsieur Gauguin,** Collection N. Podgourski, San Antonio, Texas. **Grape Harvest in Arles - Human Misery,** Private Collection, Zurich. **Breton Seaweed Collectors,** Museum Folkwang, Essen. **Breton Landscape with Haystack,** National Gallery of Art, Washington. **The Conversation,** State Hermitage, St. Petersburg. **The Meal or The Bananas,** Musee d'Orsay, Paris. **The Woodcutter or Man with an Axe, Collection,** Mr. and Mrs Alexander Lewyt, New York. **Pape Moe (Mysterious Waters),** Private Collection, Zurich. **Breton Women,** Musee d'Orsay, Paris. **Mahana no atau (Day of the God),** Art Institute, Chicago. **Nave Nave Moe (Delicious Water),** State Hermitage, St Petersburg. **Portrait of young girl, Jeanne Goupil,** Ordrupgaardsamlingen, Copenhagen. **Te Vaa (The Canoe),** Collection M.A. Morosov, State Hermitage, St Petersburg. **Where are we from? What are we? Where are we going?,** Museum of Fine Arts, Boston. **The Ford or the Flight,** Pushkin Museum, Moscow. **Primitive Tales,** Museum Folkwang, Essen. **Still Life with Parrots,** Pushkin Museum, Moscow. **Young Woman with Fan,** Museum Folkwang, Essen.

OTHER TITLES IN THIS SERIES

ILLUMINATED MANUSCRIPTS

ALLEN JONES

CELTIC ART

SALVADOR DALI

HOKUSAI

PRE-RAPHAELITES

CASPAR DAVID FRIEDRICH

First published in Great Britain in 1997 by **Brockhampton Press**
20 Bloomsbury Street, London WC1B 3QA
a member of the **Hodder Headline Group**

ISBN 1 86019 492 3
A copy of the CIP data is available from the British Library upon request.

Designed and produced for **Brockhampton Press**
by Keith Pointing Design Consultancy.
Text written by Rosemary Pointing MA

All pictures courtesy of AKG London.

Printed and Bound in Italy by L.E.G.O. Spa.